didyahavadaddy

DIDYAHAVADADDY

A book by

Daniel Isaac Morris

VICOA.COM
Pennsylvania, USA

ISBN-10 0982825013
ISBN-13 9780982825013

"The father is always a Republican toward his son, and his mother's always a Democrat." — Robert Frost

"One father is more than a hundred schoolmasters." — George Herbert

"My father didn't tell me how to live; he lived, and let me watch him do it." — Clarence Budington Kelland

Daniel Isaac Morris, has written three novels:

"Grave Creek Conspiracy" is the sequel to Morris' first book *"Grave Creek Connections,"* a mystery set in the tri-county region of Greene/Washington County, in Pennsylvania, and in Marshall County, West Virginia. The story ties up some loose ends of a police investigation of the disappearance of college co-eds whose bodies are found in the near-by game hunting lands. But it leaves the reader with enough mystery to stir his/her imagination and perhaps, a Grave Creek franchise.

"Swaypole" reveals more West Virginia quirks and is his newest work. Set in the mythical retirement community of Gibsonton, West Virginia. The town is inhabited by mafia dons, ex-CIA, FBI along with some other ex-public officials—or so it seems.

"Cheat River" is set along the Cheat in northeastern West Virginia, not that far from the mean streets of the D.C./Baltimore/Philadelphia urban sprawl. At the source of the Cheat a couple of nefarious characters have set up a processing plant to accommodate the hit men operating in the northeast and that's not all…

The books are available at local bookstores and the usual online booksellers. For a preview and synopsis, visit http://www.dimorris.com

You are a child of the universe no less than the trees and the stars; you have a right to be here. And whether or not it is clear to you, no doubt the universe is unfolding as it should...

With all its sham, drudgery, and broken dreams, it is still a beautiful world. Be cheerful. Strive to be happy." —Max Ehrmann

FORWARD

Even for those who had the advantage of a father, it was often a
father in name only. In fact, most have not had a "traditional" daddy
in the pre-21st Century sense. Or perhaps better yet, a WWII or pre-
Woodstock era role model.

All of us undoubtedly have had a daddy…somewhere. However, many don't have one now. Given the fact that single-parent
homes and out-of-wedlock births have soared in the past couple of
decades, many children haven't had the advantage of a male role
model in their lives. This isn't to say all fathers of the post Korean
War universe are losers; it is to say that many children have not been
provided a basic moral compass or value system that is necessary
for their survival. Some have, but to point them out is to make the
argument. Consequently, fifty percent of all Hispanic kids, seventy
percent of black children have no daddy and half of all marriages end
in divorce. Evidence of this widespread fatherlessness is revealed in
crime, violence, drug and alcohol abuse, dropout rates, gang mem-
bership, and explosive jail and prison populations.

Those who have or had fathers often got a candy-coated version of
how things are. "My boy might grow up to be president. With hard
work, all things are possible." You may have been told that everyone
deserves a caring society that will somehow take care of you from
the cradle to the grave.

A certain amount of optimism is a good thing, but it must also
be tempered with a helping of the truth. Post-WWII folks have a

difficult time dealing with simple truths if they don't fit their precon-
ceived optimistic notions.

Some mothers have been able to provide a values structure for
their children, but mothers have a different motivation and separate
methods of child rearing than do their fathers. Like it or not, there are
two different genders with entirely different operational modes. The
claims that there are no gender differences are patently and demon-
strably ridiculous and not worthy of argument. Nearly one-fourth
of all children under age 15 are raised without a father and nearly a
third of their mothers were never married.

In homes in which two parents raise the children, the father is
often belabored with one or more part-time, or even full-time, jobs.
Many children are figuratively or literally fatherless.

In the years since Woodstock, Western culture has worked very
hard to divorce itself from values and judgments. Academe has set
the tone by requiring values-neutral, values clarification courses in
public schools and colleges—often funded by government grants.

The rejection of values is indicated by recent comments made by a
mother who refused to make judgments. She didn't want to condemn
a convicted rapist-murderer of children because, as she said, "I don't
want to appear to be judgmental." In another example, a well-known
politician said he didn't want to be judgmental when it came to how
a mass-murdering dictator who tortured his people should be treated.
He didn't want to speak ill of Saddam Hussein.

These attitudes of permissiveness, of not being judgmental, and
not being able to make prudent life decisions, permeate the culture.
Unfortunately, life requires us to make these sorts of judgments on a
daily basis and many of us are ill-prepared to make them.

Much is made of common sense. Common sense is as likely to
fail as often as scientific evidence if the person making the decision
isn't prepared to use both. Common sense may lead you to believe
a crumpled piece of paper will fall more slowly than a cannon ball,

but anyone who knows Newton's law knows they both fall at equal speed.

Common sense has no claim on truth or the right way of doing things. It's simply one of the tools we may use in analyzing a situation; it's not the be all and end all. That said, there are many out there who have no common sense at all. Moreover, they see no need for it.

One example is talk show host Rosie O'Donnell's contention that there is no difference between Islamic terrorism and Christianity. This is called moral equivalency. (A, Islamic terrorists who value violence, war, killing, torture, and suicide are the moral equivalent of B, Christians who value peace, love, and understanding.) According to O'Donnell, there is no difference and they are therefore equal. These people point to a few aberrations of violent Christian history to support their arguments.

Moral equivalency is not the strong suit of current liberals. They can see no distinction between a terrorist and a soldier. They both engage in violent combat and they are therefore equal. Never mind the soldier is bound by rules of engagement, has to wear a uniform, and is obligated to use force only when necessary. The uniformed soldier is held accountable for his actions. Moreover, the soldier's duty is to avoid collateral damage and civilian casualties as best the battlefield allows. The intention is to defeat the armed forces they are opposing. Any variation in the soldier's approach to his duty can and will be met with appropriate punishment. However, this isn't to say all misbehaving soldiers are punished.

They point to exceptional behavior such as the aberrant Abu Ghraib case in which a few Americans tortured prisoners as indicative of all of the American military.

On the other hand, the terrorist attempts to have his way by whatever violent means are available. The essence of terrorism is to inflict as much suffering as possible without regard to duty or any obligation outside of prevailing. The intention is to defeat the people they oppose by inflicting as much death and damage as possible—and using any means.

Some try to make the case of America as a terrorist nation, much like terrorist states we have opposed. Since WWI, in every case that this nation has taken up arms, it has been to defend itself or its allies. In World War II or subsequent wars, we have never "conquered" foreign territory nor annexed it or even colonized it. The defeated Axis Powers enjoyed the restoration of their countries and benefited from a measure of democracy and freedom they had not known before. We may leave troops in defeated lands to protect the peace, but we do not occupy defeated countries as conquerors.

It is as if the post '60s generation was taught the fine art of fallacious argument. Any post-Dr. Spock discourse is typically an exercise in which every fallacy is demonstrated.

Let's look at cause and effect for a moment. You've been taught some erroneous things about cause and effect. Forget those and pay attention. As an example, if we spend more on teacher's salaries, student grades will go up. Of course this premise is ridiculous, but we hear it time and time again, "If we would only spend more on education, education would improve." There is absolutely no proof that one will cause the other. In fact there is far more evidence to the contrary.

But that isn't the point of this book. The point is to offer some advice. Like all advice, it's presented for whatever value it has. Take it or leave it.

* * * *

In the movie, *A Few Good Men*, after Tom Cruise tells Jack Nicholson he wants the truth, Jack shouts at Tom, "You can't handle the truth!"

John 8:32 – Then you will know the truth, and the truth will set you free.

No one wants to destroy your dreams but if you want them to

grow you will have to have a fundamental understanding of the truth. You must also know that the truth is a very, very slippery commodity.

CAN YOU HANDLE THE TRUTH?

Don't assume that because you read it or heard it from so-called experts that it is the truth. Find it for yourself but base it on evidence and rational thought and never emotion. Strive to have a good time. Old folks used to encourage younger people to "sow your wild oats," whatever that meant. The problem today is there are just too many ways to be killed or maimed for life. Above all, be careful out there.

1. Everyone does not believe it, no matter what you've been told.

Much of what follows in this book is based on recognizing this fundamental fallacy. Anyone who wants to exploit you (this includes just about anyone you can imagine) knows you want to belong. You want to fit in. You want to be part of a group.

Get over it. Don't be gullible, don't be a dupe, and stand up for yourself. If the best reasoning you can get from someone is that everybody is doing it, or that's what everyone says or believes, begin right there to question what they are telling you.

Even authority figures, clergymen, teachers, professors, and others may not offer you good advice or legitimate information. There are enough cases in which authority figures abuse their influence to make anyone suspicious.

Above all, be suspicious of the "herd." There is a famous instance in which students were asked who Martin Luther was. Every student but one answered Martin Luther was an illustrious civil rights leader who was assassinated in 1968.

Some still angrily defended their answer even when they were proven wrong. Since you are reading this book, you probably know the civil rights leader who was shot by James Earl Ray was Martin Luther King, Junior. Martin Luther was a priest and the theologian who initiated the Protestant Reformation.

Remember, you can take a poll or vote on anything you like, but a majority opinion may not necessarily find the truth. No matter what the herd said, no matter what their opinion was, Martin Luther was not Martin Luther King.

The word "niggardly" is an adjective meaning stingy or miserly.

Because it "sounds" like the dreaded "N" word, an aide to the mayor of Washington, D.C. was attacked for using it because ignorant people thought it was a racial slur. So much for herd-thinking. So much for intelligence. Being a member of a minority doesn't make you any more right than being in the majority.

A continuing theme in this book is "think for yourself." You have direct access to the greatest sources of information the world has known. The Internet and television provide more information than all of the accumulated knowledge of any given person or institution. Like anything, these media must be used with caution and common sense. But you will learn more watching the History Channel for a few hours a week than you will ever learn in any history course. This isn't to suggest that information on the History Channel is never flawed or biased. All information should be open to question.

Never has the old excuse of ignorance been more pitiful.

2. Lying and lying liars

Many of the people you don't know personally, and some that you do, will lie to you. This is something you may not believe or something you may wish to avoid. However, deception, deceit, and duplicity are the stuff of politics, advertising, and business. Check out some print or other media advertising sometime.

Keeping you in the dark and keeping you naïve and gullible are in the best interest of those who make a living duping you. Education should be the antidote to all of this foolery, but ask yourself, when was the last time you were given information about how economics work, how to figure out a basic mortgage, how to use and balance a checkbook, or what the real costs of having a credit card might be?

Isn't that a crass, awful thing to say? There are people who will deceive and take advantage of you? Okay, try this. Advertisers are often required to put a disclaimer in their advertising—so they can say, we told you so. You should have read it. Now try to read the disclaimer at the end of one of those TV commercials, or the one at the bottom of the screen. If you can actually freeze the frame and have a big-enough screen, it makes for some pretty interesting reading.

Or, try this one. Order one of the free products that ask you to "Pay only shipping and handling." Compare what you paid for shipping and handling with the actual cost of handling and shipping it. Compare the value of the "free" product with what you paid.

You probably have never encountered the realities of interest and how much it might cost you to pay off a 30-year loan. A typical loan on a $150,000 house will cost you nearly $350,000 by the time you pay it off. This doesn't include the extras—closing costs, taxes, utilities, maintenance, association dues, insurance, and the other "normal" costs of home ownership. You can begin to see why this sort of stuff isn't mentioned much in school.

Be very careful if your history teacher tells you America stole the Indians' land or that Columbus didn't discover America or a whole ration of other half-truths.

For what it's worth, much of the land early settlers developed was simply there for the taking. At that time, (remember "at that time" for later reference) few indigenous people in the new world had any conception of land ownership. When Manhattan was "bought" from the Indians at a very low price, the Indians thought they were ripping off the new guys on the block. They counted their loot and chuckled because they knew that neither they, nor anyone else, had title to the land they had just sold. Of course the Indians—now known as "Native" Americans—didn't have to have Columbus to "discover" where they lived. Columbus discovered the New World as far as Europeans were concerned. And, it was his "discovery" that led to the European settlement of America.

This isn't to say American's didn't steal Native American land. They did when land ownership became more formalized. This isn't to say Native American rights weren't abused by the Government and Europeans. Their rights were abused and many died as a result. Wounded Knee, Sand Creek and Washita are only tiny spots on a series of blots making up the tapestry of American History. The massacres may have ended, but the abuses have not.

By the way, a "Native American" is anyone born in America. The ancestors of the "Native Americans"—Indians or indigenous people, to be politically correct—came from elsewhere. According to one theory, all of us came from Africa, so we may all be African-Americans. Confusing, ain't it? The politically correct prefer it that way.

Some of the most dangerous and devious deceptions are the ones that have an element of truth. Recently some college professors have sucked their students into believing fabrications concerning the history of America using a technique called revisionist history.

For example, we are told that early America's founding fathers were evil because they were slaveholders. This has a spark of truth about it because slaveholding is evil and it is a fact that some early Americans were slaveholders. However, the charge of evil-doer must be taken with a grain of salt.

Our culture, our society—in our time and place—sees slavery for what it is, clearly evil. However, at the time of the founders, slavery was legal and some of them were slave owners. This doesn't make it moral or ethical in our view, but it does require a modicum of understanding.

At that time slaves were considered property much the same way that other things were owned. Although abolitionists warned against it, owning slaves was legal, people did it and saw nothing wrong with it. It took intelligent, informed people to recognize the evil of slavery.

To instill white guilt and perpetuate the half-truth concept of racism, Black Liberation Theologians and racial victim-ologists won't tell you that blacks owned more than 10,000 slaves in Louisiana, Maryland, South Carolina, and Virginia. Some black slaveholders owned slaves for beneficent reasons, but only a few history profs will tell you that the black slave owners bred and sold slaves as well. Admittedly, black slave ownership wasn't common, but then neither was white ownership of slaves. Statistically, slave owners made up a small minority of the population. Makes it kind of tough to decide who might get reparations, doesn't it?

By the way, whipping and punishing slaves was relatively rare as well. Even a cruel slave-owner might think twice about disabling "property" he had acquired at great expense. You might see a free white man tied to a whipping post as often as a black slave.

Native Americans were seen as ignorant, "Godless" savages without the capacity to understand the civilized world. Indians were construed as heathens that needed to be saved by Christians. This common misconception led to their mistreatment and exploitation.

Some early settlers called the Indians "Thieving Savages" because they took things that didn't belong to them. Never mind that the concepts of property and ownership were unknown to the "savage." He was simply taking what he needed, as he had always done.

We cannot make judgments about people who lived in other times at other places, using morals and values that did not apply in their time.

Astonishingly, many of America's heroes and historic figures are maligned because they didn't follow the politically correct "moral" codes of the 21st Century.

It's silly to imagine someone chastising a pioneer for cutting a tree or reminding him that we should save our forests for future generations when he was surrounded by trees and needed open fields to plant crops that he could eat.

3. Learn how to argue

From time to time all of us have to convince others about some point or other. No, this is not the griping you typically do. Learn how to convince someone that you have a valid point of view, one they might want to consider. You won't be taught how to argue by your liberal or progressive friends and college professors. Their arguments more often than not consist of descriptions of what they feel or, as they will blatantly tell you, "this is my opinion." When someone is trying to convince you of their point of view, take notice of the times they talk about their own personal feelings or what "everyone says."

A good arguer, or a good lawyer, employs evidence to make their point. Logic, reason, and understanding are the bases of sound arguments. They are also the antithesis of liberal, romantic thought.

Most schools used to have debate teams—a few still do. Teams of students were taught how to argue effectively. Many talented lawyers were brought to that profession by participating in debates. One might suspect that the demise of debate teams was purposeful. It seems educationalists don't want rational or logical questioning of their values.

There are some people you should never argue with because they aren't interested in your point of view. Among them are drunks. "Never argue with a drunk" is sage advice. You aren't going to convince him of anything and he may just convince you to join him in a drink.

4. Don't get involved in arguments about religion

All of us have encountered folks who have found "The Way," whether they come in pairs, come knocking on your door on Saturday morning, or you meet them at the family reunion. Do not engage these people in an argument. Their intention is to show you "Their Way" and to offer it to you as salvation. They are not interested in your way or your ideas.

If you have a strong foundation in your faith, no one is going to talk you into becoming a (insert whatever faith you choose). Why? It's simple. Your faith isn't a matter to be proven with logic, reason, or understanding, it's something you simply accept. "It's a matter of faith," which is to say that whatever it is, or how you can define it, you accept and believe it.

For example: I may believe that fuzzy things crawl out of the woodwork at night and offer me salvation. If I truly believe this and it's my faith, there is nothing you can do to dissuade me. There is no logic you can use to make me believe my fuzzies are figments of my—or someone else's—imagination. Historic or scientific evidence is relatively useless when attacking or defending one's faith.

Above all, don't argue with zealots or fundamentalists. These are the folks who are so convinced they have "The Way" that they will do anything to make you accept their version of the "truth." They don't want your tolerance or your reasoned consideration. Some fundamentalists are so insistent that their way is the one true way that they will even kill to get others to see the world as they see it.

Television personality Bill Maher constantly refers to religion as bunk. Of course Mr. Maher doesn't understand that religion is not what can or cannot be proven, it is what you choose to believe. Little does he understand—no matter how much he wishes it were so—he cannot tell you what to believe.

5. You can't negotiate with someone who doesn't want anything.

One of the most obvious faults of current discourse is the concept that diplomacy and negotiation will result in understanding and peace.

"We gave up on diplomacy too soon," is the cry of those who hate the Iraq war. President Barrack Obama wants to negotiate with the world's despots and says he will meet with them unconditionally.

Imagine, if you will, that you are trying to sell your idea to a businessman. The businessman isn't interested, and your idea has no appeal for him. Moreover, he has developed a life-long hatred for you and has no interest in you or anything you are selling. Makes for a pretty tough sell, doesn't it?

The current crop of Islamic fascists don't want riches. They either have everything or nothing. Islamic fundamentalists are not the least concerned with materialism—unlike Westerners—and they aren't concerned with the here and now. They are, rather, concerned with the hereafter. If you had a history teacher, you might know this is a medieval concept.

For them, the ultimate reality is in the afterlife. Life on earth has little meaning. Imagine living in a mud hut or cave with little in the way of possessions and you might see their point. The only thing they want is for you to die, or submit to their religion and live under their rule as they see it defined in their law (Sharia). Makes for a pretty tough sell, doesn't it?

So, normal diplomacy or negotiation such as, you give me this point, I'll forego that point, doesn't work in this marketplace. Across the table sits a person who wants nothing and will never give up

23

anything. Negotiate? You have to be kidding.

6. Listen to your friends, relatives, and parents' opinions about who you fall in love with.

If they are telling you to go easy with your relationship with the person who's beating you up on weekends and using drugs daily, think things over. The correct reply here isn't "But I love him/her" or "He/she will change."

If enough of this cautionary advice is presented, you would do well to consider the sources and examine your motives very carefully. Right now, you may not be sane enough to dump the typical creep. Wait a while, let the hormones settle, and take a look through new eyes.

If worst comes to worst, check out some of the losers that some of your friends who may have been less than aware came up with.

25

7. Moviegoers beware—film is a business, not an art form.

Unfortunately, filmmakers learned very early on that profits are more likely to be made by re-making, redoing, and regurgitating works that have a track record. *Frankenstein*, fifty-one times, *Dracula*, forty-three versions and counting (pun intended), and there are over sixty versions of *A Christmas Carol*.

Many of these were made before the last few decades of film decadence. One artist describes decadence as "when art turns back and feeds upon itself."

Since the 1950s, filmmakers have relied on the new bastard (television) for material to be exploited for regurgitation. As this is written, numerous spin-offs from television series are common fare for theater marquees. (The hottest film of the 2008 summer was the fourth remake of *Indiana Jones and the...*whatever.)

The righteous "artistes" will decry any hint of plagiarism while at the same time "creating" film after film with the same plot or theme. "Creature created by science gone wrong," or "celestial object hits earth," and "costumed heroes fight crime," have been done ad nauseam. By the way, why would a person in the future who has unlimited technology, stun guns, ray guns, atomic cannons, trilithium resin, or a Vulcan nerve pinch ever choose to fight with a sword, or any other sharp and pointy thing?

The problem isn't the lack of new, or even exotic material for films. With word processors on every desktop there is no paucity of scripts or written material. The problem is good old American capitalistic greed.

The parallel, of course, is books in whatever form. Novelists—

even the best of James Patterson and Stephen King and their surro-
gates—churn out words that are commercial if not art. Patterson and
this writer openly admit, their words are not "art." Romance novels
pollute the shelves of bookstores not because they offer anything
new. They provide the familiar, and the intent and the goal of the
publishers is profit.

Where film is concerned, there is little chance that a film, even
real stinkers like *Porky's* or *Revenge of the Nerds* remakes, won't
give their backers a return on their money. They are released for a
brief appearance in theaters. The faithful will go just to see if it's like
the first one. Then on to disc (in the old days, it was tape.) Next to
cable, then to the Internet for another money wringing, then to the
foreign markets, and finally to broadcast TV. But we're not done yet.
By this time the dogs are ready to be recycled through the discount
disc, Internet release, replay-on-cable markets. Tune through your
viewers' guide sometime and note the number of movies you have
never seen that are playing on the "free" movie channels.

All along the way, nickels and dimes are picked up, the movie
is paid off and backers cash in on the dregs. An unsuccessful film
makes only millions; successful ones make hundreds of millions.

Do not subscribe to cable "premium" movie channels. All of the
good movie channels are free with a good cable subscription. If you
insist on one of the so-called "premium" channels try it for about
three months.

New offerings are as rare as a real plot in a Kung Fu movie.
Your brief exposure to a "premium" channel will provide you
with an opportunity to see all of the old movies on the free
channels and a couple of new ones over and over again—usually
the rotten ones that couldn't make it elsewhere. After you have
fulfilled your foolish fantasies of unlimited reruns of *Beast-
master*, *Dirty Dancing*, and *Ferris Bueller's Day Off*, you may
decide to do irreparable harm to yourself or end it all by watch-

27

ing *Mom and Dad Save the World*, one more time.

(It's one of my all time favorite schlock flicks. It has yet to achieve true cult status, but just wait.)

8. Taxes

Presidential candidate Barrack Obama promised that anyone making under $250 thousand would not pay any additional taxes. Or was that $200 thousand? Or maybe it was $150 thousand. By now you know it doesn't matter what the promises are, you will pay.

You have probably seen some of the eighteen-wheelers going down the highway with signs proclaiming how much they pay in taxes. Like the politicians, they are lying to you. Neither the trucks, nor the corporations who own them, pay taxes.

Leftists will mount their soapboxes and preach to the ignorant how the government should tax big corporations and hand out money to the poor. They never bother to explain that corporations—that means businesses to leftists—don't pay taxes.

Anyone selling a product or service factors in the cost of producing that product or service when determining the price they will charge. Taxes and fees are a part of the cost of doing business.

Imagine you are selling a glass of lemonade. You are paying for lemons, water, sugar, and other incidental costs of producing your product. You charge a dollar for a glass of your lemonade. Along comes the government and tells you they are going to tax your lemonade at ten cents a glass. If you are a smart businessperson, you will raise the price by ten cents, so you can stay even. If you are a sharp businessperson, you will raise the price twenty cents and blame your price increase on the government.

It's all too obvious, only the consumers pay taxes. Moreover, the spread-the-wealth scheme won't work because those who will have to pay are already figuring out how they can avoid taxes.

It might sound good to someone living in low-income housing that energy corporations are going to be taxed. However, by this time you should realize your energy costs are going to go up.

When a politician, such as Obama, claims he or she won't raise your taxes, they are typically talking about the graduated income tax. In fact, most people don't pay income tax at all. The bottom half of wage earners pay only three percent of the total income taxes collected. The top one percent pays forty percent of the tax bill.

The nation is in a Mobius loop of taxing and spending. There can never be enough taxes because inflation—the cost of living (COLA)—is built into government employee agreements, Social Security, and other contracts. So, the need for more money is built into the system. If that isn't bad enough, politicians who want to ensure re-election, spend more each year on projects in their home states while all of Congress dreams up new schemes to spend money.

Politicians lie about cutting costs. They pretend to cut services such as police, schools, healthcare, Social Security, etc. until people scream for them to stop cutting. Then, they raise taxes, fees, surcharges, permits...you get the picture.

The problem with spreading the wealth by way of the graduated income tax is that it's not the only method of collecting revenue. There are state income taxes, sales taxes, property taxes, and literally hundreds of other taxes, fees, surcharges, etc. that are too numerous to list.

9. Beware of the brain rinse.

If you went to college, it may be too late. Colleges—including the ones that claim university status—openly admit that their faculties consist of a majority of liberal-progressives. A neo-con conservative is as rare on a college campus as pork at a Jewish barbecue. (I know, insensitive.)

Colleges openly invite radicals of the left to have discussions with their students. This is to further their abilities to reason, to think, and to provide diversity of thought. Additionally, it demonstrates the concept of free speech.

To prove they have assimilated these skills, college students openly oppose other points of view and discourage diverse thought by shouting down speakers and throwing pies. (Speech should only be free if you agree with me.) "Exotic" thinkers, they believe, should not sully their quest for someone to provide enlightenment by reinforcing their bigoted ideas.

One of the goals of the so-called liberal minds is to make sure you are not exposed to other modes of thought. "Pure" thinkers, who abide nothing less than purity, will surround you and you must believe and agree with those with whom you associate or be ostracized. They know that given enough of their indoctrination, you will eventually become one of them. Your brain will be rinsed of unorthodox thought and you will "fit in." You will escape being labeled and become a good member of the herd. No one wants to be left out.

The most virulent racist, bigoted, anti-American, left wing, socialist/communist-fascist will find a home and perhaps a tenured professorship at your local hall of academe where he/she will be protected and defended on grounds of academic freedom and freedom of speech. On the other hand, a bigoted, right-wing, Nazi-fascist, skin-headed, KKK member will be excoriated, condemned, and fired. No academic freedom, no free speech for him/her. Check the politics of the president and his/her tenured professors sometime.

Educate yourself. You will learn what you need to know and what you want to know — not what others want you to know.

If you want a few good chuckles ask one of your professors to discuss the illegal alien problem in America. If he corrects your use of "illegal alien" and tells you they are undocumented immigrants — just sit back and enjoy the ride.

10. Learn to cook.

Sometime after age eighteen you will learn that Mickey Dee's might supply great toys and trinkets, but so far as food goes, they are a disaster. Most restaurant food will taste like—well—restaurant food. Which is to say, boring. Why boring? Because it's made to suit everyone's taste. I know people who like black beans on chocolate cake and jelly on hamburgers. In Cincinnati, Ohio, nearly the entire city loves chili that contains chocolate and cinnamon. They even eat the concoction on spaghetti. With that sort of stuff in the "everyone's taste" pool, you can begin to see why eating out will eventually become...boring.

Don't become caught in the trap of buying pre-prepared and packaged food. This is the same quality, or worse, than restaurant food. In fact, some packages of this stuff often carry restaurant labels. No matter what your friends say, cooking is not gender specific. There are thousands, perhaps millions of both men and women around the world that are highly skilled and qualified cooks.

Television cooking shows are a joke. The meal the cook is making is prepared and proportioned in advance by slave labor. (Can you say intern?) The cook does a little pretend cutting, measuring, and dumping stuff in bowls, but there is little cooking going on. This mess is popped into an oven or onto a stove that no real person can afford, then for "the sake of time," it appears fully cooked from another part of the set. If you want the recipe for the meal, you have to buy the cook/actor's book.

To learn to cook, get a decent recipe book to start. The formulas contained in it are not engraved in stone and, after some experience, change the amounts and ingredients to suit yourself.

Make friends with a person whose food you like. Get them to share their secrets and concoctions with you. Avoid the ones that make their recipes and cooking a big secret. They selfishly guard their cooking so everyone will love only them.

Remember, the idea is for you to be able to create something that is tasty, nutritious, and inexpensive. Aside from being boring, restaurant food is expensive. In eating establishments, you have to pay for the whole operation in addition to what you are eating.

11. Do not engage in discussions about race.

This is particularly true if your race is in the majority. Before I continue, let's recognize that because I just wrote the sentence above, I have, no doubt, been labeled a "racist." The term is so hackneyed, so over-used, that it has become meaningless. The definition of a racist is "anyone who believes in the superiority of his or her own particular race."

In a recent clash between two Caucasian groups, the press referred to the incident as a racist struggle. In case you haven't guessed, the bad guys were the racists.

Could it be that those who are taught their race is beautiful and have racial pride, are being taught racism? Perhaps it could be true if they are members of the Nazi youth, but never if they are members of a minority. Minority groups are often taught that their own group cannot be—by definition—racist.

More recently the racist label has come to include non-racial groups and ethnic groups exclusive of race. Let's put it this way, any discussion of ethnicity, national origin, or race will bring charges of racism. Do not question this, you can't win and you will be labeled a racist.

12. Do not express your beliefs about the morality of homosexuality.

To begin, this is another area in which much of the English language has been co-opted by those who promote the homosexual agenda. Americans fear being labeled almost as much as they fear AIDS and other sexually transmitted diseases. Being labeled a homophobe is nearly akin to being labeled a racist.

Homo, in this instance does not have anything to do with the Latin word for man. Homo in this case is the Greek word for "same." Homophobe simply means same-fear, or fear of folks of the same gender. To move the homosexual agenda of acceptance forward, homosexuals have declared that a homophobe is anyone who disagrees with their program of acceptance. However, seldom does anyone who is labeled a homophobe fear homosexuals, they simply oppose their lifestyle on moral or whatever grounds.

Ergo, homophobes (sounds like some despicable life form) are evil and are to be attacked. On the other hand, homosexuals have co-opted the word gay to mean homosexual. Homosexual sounds much like what it is—a person who has sex with a person of the same gender. Gay equals good and, therefore, describes a fun, exciting person. Homophobe equals bad—an evil life form.

Gays will not go away. They don't want you to merely tolerate their choices of sexual partners, they want you to accept them. They don't just want acceptance, they prefer that you join with them.

Miss California in 2009 expressed an opinion held by the majority of Californians and the President of the United States. She had the temerity to say she opposed gay marriage. She was excoriated, called names, and removed from the position of Miss California.

So, you see, if you express any opinion involving race or homosexuality, or nearly any liberal-opposed opinion, you are racist and a homophobe—as well as politically incorrect and insensitive.

13. Don't listen to anyone who proposes all people should be equal.

If you think this one over it should be obvious to anyone that it isn't a very good idea. It's one of those naïve, simplistic concepts that sounds so noble and romantic until it is thought through.

In terms of the rest of the world, no matter how poor an American you may be, you are infinitely wealthy. If you look at the average third world citizen, you will see someone who is undoubtedly living in abject poverty. Interestingly enough, the people are living under an over-class who could improve their lot, but are not progressive enough to do so.

Poverty is a word without meaning to Americans. When we think of "the poor," we think of people with only a few thousand dollars worth of goods, people who rely on a few thousand a year for subsistence, people who are given clothing and the necessities of life. We cannot envision a person who has nothing—who in some cases actually eats starch mixed with dirt to stave off hunger.

Given the way the world works, the distribution of the world's limited resources, real equality, is in all probability, impossible. However, if true parity could be accomplished, those who demand equality would be the first to complain or somehow escape equity.

For equality to happen, the day-to-day working American would have to give up much of what they enjoy in material goods and income and live a day-to-day existence on the edge of starvation, just to make things equal and fair.

Equality is only possible if all are equally impoverished and miserable. Sorry, but the world's resources just won't allow everyone to be rich. Of course this isn't what the liberal/socialists/statists have in mind for you. They just want the world to be fair. To those who want equality, they want it for you. Deep in their own hearts, they believe they will somehow rise above it.

Their ignorance of economics and the laws of distribution lead them to believe that all the world's people could be wealthy. After all, all Americans are wealthy.

Your grandparent(s) lived their entire lives hearing about the starving people of the third world, particularly Africa. Not much has changed for those people during the past sixty years.

It's an inescapable fact that if everyone in the world suddenly became wealthy, those at the bottom of the economic ladder would still be poor.

14. Know that populist politicians lie. (Of course they do, all politicians lie.)

It's not that they mean to, or that they aren't well intentioned, they just have to tell lies to get elected. In an unusual moment of candor, a Democrat revealed he had to lie about ending the war in Iraq to get elected. He said he knew full well the Democrats could not end the war.

The first lie: Populist politicians claim they are working for the working class. No they aren't, they are in it for themselves. They want a position and they want power, prestige, and perks. Ask any of the current crop if they would like to place limits on their term of office. If they love the working class, they should be willing to step aside and let some others try it for a while.

The next lie: Populist politicians claim to be plain folks, just like you. No they aren't. Most of them never had a job. They went to Harvard, Yale, or some other college you could never afford and got a law degree. Those who might have had a job, worked behind a desk thinking great thoughts and shuffling large amounts of paper. They never were a person like you, making an average wage, working by the sweat of your brow, a person who could never afford to run for office. Most have never run a business—even a popsicle shop.

In 2008 three people ran and ran, seemingly forever. They went from town to town, state to state, and interview after interview for months on end. The three were John McCain, Hillary Clinton, and Barrack Obama. Fortunately they didn't have jobs that required them to be present to collect a paycheck and keep their positions. In every instance, they were senators. Obviously, senators or other political office holders don't work. Do you really think you could afford to take off work to campaign for office? They lied to you. They aren't just plain folks and they don't have the remotest idea what is required to hold a job or to be an ordinary person.

The presidential candidate couples in 2008 had incomes in the millions of dollars. Just having one million dollars in a savings account could net you $50,000 in interest for one year without ever having to lift a finger or touch your million. Does this sound like your standard of living?

One of the greatest myths is that the Democrats are the party of the people and the Republicans are the party of business. Balderdash, this is campaign rhetoric that is trotted out during election time. Once elected both parties become the parties of the politicians—until the next election. If the party they are elected into dumps them—or they dump it—they move on to another one. Ask Arlen Specter or Joe Lieberman.

15. Fair

A fair is a place with clowns, Ferris wheels, cattle shows, and lots of monkey poop and scam artists. Fair is something that may be enforced by grade school teachers for a short time but it is a concept abandoned in the teen years and early adult life. It may reappear sometime in an afterlife, but not now. Get used to the idea, nothing is fair. No one will tell you this, it just isn't something they think you should hear.

An improvised explosive device in Kheyl, Afghanistan, killed Lt. Brian Bradshaw, 24, a 2007 graduate of Pacific Lutheran University. This was the same day that a famous celebrity died of, apparently, a drug misadventure.

The House of Representatives declared a moment of silence and President Barrack Obama wrote a personal note of condolence to the family—for the celebrity, an entertainer.

This was the House of Representatives that sent Bradshaw into harm's way and the President who was his Commander in Chief who ordered him to the battlefield. It's the sort of fairness you should get used to if you intend to live in the real world.

16. Stereotyping

You have been led to believe that stereotyping is an indication of ignorance and bigotry and that it is to be avoided by intelligent people. Again, you are being misled. Stereotyping is a handy tool for living a long life, if it's used with caution and common sense.

"See that bum over there?" See, like I said, "stereotyping." Because the poor man has not had a bath, is covered with needle tracks, is unshaven, wearing torn and filthy clothing, and is nodding off, you have made assumptions about him that may not be valid. You have stereotyped him, or as your professor might put it, you have made an association of variables that are loosely if at all correlated.

Doesn't work for you, huh? Can't tell anything given the information you have? Let's add one more thing—the poor fellow is your new gynecologist—or perhaps your new defense attorney?

You've heard about "profiling?" This is what the politically correct would equate with stereotyping. Stereotyping equals bad, profiling equals bad.

If you are involved in security screening you might want to keep in mind current terrorists more often than not are—by a vast majority—Muslims. Furthermore, they are, by a vaster majority, between the ages of 17 and 35. By a larger majority, they are male.

Politically correct extremists would have you believe you should ignore young, adult, Muslim men and direct your attention to everyone. Ignoring these folks hasn't worked for the Israelis and other security officers that have an ounce of common sense, but we insist Americans avoid profiling. In your personal life, use stereotyping and profiling to stay safe. Don't tell anyone you are doing this or you will be labeled... Ooooh.

You are at the racetrack and you notice that nearly—not always, but nearly always—the horse that wins is large, brown, and has white feet. What will the next horse that you bet on look like? You stereotyping profiler you.

17. Dope—did its use cause an incident?

Put what you've been told aside, all dope is dangerous. If it were otherwise, no one would want it. Don't believe that there are no "gateway" drugs either. By a very vast majority (think about your friends), marijuana users were, or still are, tobacco smokers. Tobacco may well be a gateway to pot.

The brainless may suggest that cannabis users will become dope fiends (think about your friends) and you know from personal experience this isn't true. Does that mean pot is not a gateway drug? Use your common sense now. No, but it surely doesn't mean it is not a gateway either. Nearly all heroin addicts or crack heads started with something further down the dope chain. Remember cause/effect? Remember common sense?

If there is a high, beyond your "normal" experience, it follows there will come a low—when you return to your normal experience. Now if the substances you are using alter the way you experience the world, it follows that it is—at least on a temporary basis—altering your brain.

It isn't much of a leap to figure out that the more messing you do with your brain, the greater the chance of permanent alteration.

"The incident didn't involve drug use." That's a typical comment, particularly when drugs are suspected to begin with. Does this mean that when drugs are not detectable in a person, there has been no damage or brain alteration? The "didn't involve drug use" conclusion is not based on very good evidence—or evidence that is impossible to obtain. Does this mean it's true? No, but everyone may find comfort in it. A less comfortable headline might be, "The incident didn't involve CURRENT drug use."

No one—no one—knows whether previous drug use has had an effect. There is absolutely no evidence that drugs of any kind are benign and plenty of evidence they are dangerous. A short-term high isn't worth the risk—no matter what your "friends" and drug culture promoters may tell you.

The following is a list of just a few famous figures that died too young due to alcohol-drug-related deaths.

Nick Adams
Jean-Michel Basquiat
John Belushi
John Bonham
Lenny Bruce
Nick Adams
Truman Capote
Montgomery Clift
Kurt Cobain
John Entwistle
Brian Epstein
Chris Farley
Jerry Garcia
Danny Gans
Judy Garland
Andy Gibb
Mitch Hedberg
Margaux Hemingway
Jimi Hendrix
Michael Jackson
Anissa Jones
Brian Jones
Russell Jones

Janis Joplin
David Kennedy
Carole Landis
Heath Ledger
Bruce Lee
Frankie Lymon
Marilyn Monroe
Keith Moon
Jim Morrison
Chris Penn
River Phoenix
Dana Plato
Elvis Presley
Freddie Prinze
Anna Nicole Smith
Inger Stevens
Sid Vicious
Dennis Wilson...and a whole lot more.

No, drugs didn't kill all of them. Some went by their own hand—after they had messed with even sometimes legal, "substances." You, or some of those "enlightened" friends of yours, might try to explain to their families, friends, and fans how alcohol/drug abuse is harmless fun.

18. Let's legalize drugs and become a nation of idiots.

The politically correct progressives among us recommend legalization of illicit drugs. They argue that it is your body and the laws create victimless crimes that only fill prisons. It's patently obvious it's your own body and adults should be able to destroy their lives with drugs—if they are willing to fund the project. However, these folks typically want society (you and me) to fund the disasters their health and their lives become and to spend our money to bail them out.

Victimless crime? You've got to be kidding. (Think about your friends. Refer to the list of the dear departed above.) How many do you know who have family members or families that have been destroyed and their lives shattered by drug use? Insert use of common sense here. Decide for yourself, don't listen to some agency that profits by trying to legalize drugs.

The absolute best argument opposing the legalization of hard drugs is simple: It ain't gonna happen. Why? Think it through if you can.

It's MONEY, stupid. No, not the money the dope growers, drug manufactures, drug distributors, and street dealers get, although that's a factor. Money equals economy. If drugs disappeared overnight, some countries' entire economies would collapse. The largest cash crop in some states is the marijuana crop, so that economy would collapse. Literally millions of people would be deprived of a very lucrative income. And, that's just the illegal part.

The greatest losses that would impact the United States and world economies are the legal parts of the illicit drug culture.

Legal part? Yes, that's the part we'll call the misery index. This one is hard to think about because there are so many nooks and crannies that require funding, but let's examine just a few.

The entire legal/justice system is based—eighty to ninety percent by best estimates—on drug abuse. The estimate is that eighty to ninety percent of crime is drug-related. So, a significant number of those prosecutors, defense attorneys, judges, clerks, secretaries, police, investigators, sheriffs, bailiffs, communication specialists, motor pool maintenance workers, and janitors (see how complex this is?) who filter folks into the system would be out of work and no longer contributing to the economy.

Next come a number of the cleanup people who would be unemployed: doctors, nurses, counselors, sociologists, clergymen, psychologists, therapists, rehabilitators, and all of their institutions, support people, and structures. Add to these, those who provide financial support and training.

The economic impact of legalizing drugs would be staggering. The unintended and unforeseen consequences might even bring the global economy to its knees.

Separating drugs from the legal and misery-support systems just isn't possible. We have too much invested in it in time, jobs, and money.

19. Doing away with the IRS

You can file this one away in the "Ain't gonna' happen" file as well.

It's usually proposed by one of those do-gooder candidates who is "just like you." He/she is a populist politician who sees things your way. He/she is looking out for you.

The Internal Revenue Service is an easy entity for politicians to attack. Relatively few people work there and anyone who doesn't work there will support you.

Who wouldn't want to do away with a graduated income tax? Most people, when it is explained to them, would prefer a tax system based on something other than income. Something like a sales tax, or other flat tax, seems fair because it taxes everyone on what they spend.

None of these schemes will happen. Why? It's simple. The graduated income tax is the government's lever and the IRS is its fulcrum.

"Give me a lever long enough and a fulcrum on which to place it, and I shall move the world." – Archimedes

If the government wants you to make your home more energy efficient, they grant you a tax credit. If they want a corporation to produce more of what they want, they hand out a tax credit. What better way to modify behavior, what better way to exercise power?

Corporations sort of like it this way too. If you want something for your company, get a tax credit or a loophole built into the tax code you can fly an Airbus through, donate some money to a senator's campaign, and work with your lobbyist to lobby for a lucrative bridge-to-nowhere deal.

The government isn't very likely to give up its grip on power. The graduated income tax/IRS lever and fulcrum are far more powerful than anything any dictatorial despot could dream of. Don't look for a flat tax any time soon. Those who convince you a flat tax is possible may believe a flat world is possible too.

Daniel Isaac Morris

20. Self-esteem

"All you need in this life is ignorance and confidence, and then success is sure." – Mark Twain

The misbegotten idea of self-esteem is so well-worn, trite, and tired it seems useless to remind any intelligent being that the public schools and universities should attempt to eliminate it from their literature—but they won't.

Self-esteem derives from accomplishment and success. This is not an opinion or belief, it's a basic fact of life. Obtuse educationalists fell victim to cause/effect fallacy when they presumed that self-esteem can be achieved by any means other than accomplishment.

The scam: Educationalists looked at people who were successful in school and life and came to the conclusion that their accomplishments resulted in them feeling good about themselves—not achievement or even talent. They fell in love with the idea that those with self-esteem can achieve success. After all, most people with achievements feel comfortable with themselves. Conversely, the unsuccessful are dissatisfied…or as the educationalist would put it, have low self-esteem.

They loved the new concept because success might be achieved by some means other than study and hard work or engaging students in real learning. The self-esteem lovers reasoned it would be far easier to work on instilling and inculcating the new religion of self-esteem rather than engaging in the labor of teaching.

Unfortunately, as we all know, shining someone on and blowing smoke up their skirt might increase arrogance and a smug attitude but it does nothing to assure achievement or success. Studies showed that many students with high self-esteem thought they were doing much better than they actually were and conversely, those who were actually doing better, weren't so self-assured. Unfortunately, all of us don't know this. Some belated educationalists insist on cramming self-esteem into students like some would force-feed geese. The result in this case is seldom pâté and more likely excrement. If this idiocy worked, someone could tell you that you were a great actor and you would become the next Meryl Streep or Robert Di Niro.

Caution: Building up your self-esteem might lead you to a career in politics.

21. You probably will never become a celebrity.

Yes, but hundreds of people become celebrities every year.

"In the future, everyone will be world-famous for 15 minutes." – Andy Warhol

Hundreds win at Lotto but you didn't. Each year there are a few hundred winners and hundreds of millions of losers. Only a few hundred players make it into the NHL—but no one will tell you that.

No matter what your teachers and parents tell you; you aren't going to be President of the United States. Of all the millions of qualified people who have lived since this country began, only 43 have become President. (Probably not a job you would want anyway.)

Even if you stand out in a thunderstorm—a practice not advised or suggested—you probably won't be killed by lightning, although many are each year. 18,000 thunderstorms are out there 24/7, but only about 73 people are killed by them each year.

All of this goes to say the chances of you becoming a star are minimal at best, so it's no way to live your life—depending on the fact you will become a celebrity or a sports figure.

22. You aren't going to win.

Sooner or later you will go to a casino and you will lose money.
Like becoming a celebrity, it could happen that you win, but the
chances are slim to none. It is even less likely that you will win at
a place that makes its money by rigging the game so you will lose.
Casinos, racetracks, and other gambling venues are for suckers. The
theory is that the typical gambler—for a whole host of psychological
reasons—wants to lose. Likewise, the typical casino is there to offer
the gambler what he wants.

You may not be a professional gambler; you are probably a dab-
bler who has a few bucks to waste. You are caught up in the moment
and, for whatever reason, you want to contribute to the income of the
multimillionaire owners of the gambling venue. These folks will be
glad to oblige you.

It escapes most people that casinos are in business and stay in
business by making (rigging?) their "games" so the casino is more
likely to win than you are. Of course no one would play if the casino
won your money every time, so they let you win some of the time.
Psychologists call this random reinforcement.

Monkeys are trained to pull a lever and sometimes—randomly—
they get a goody. They will wear themselves out pulling the lever.
The next time you see someone at a slot machine, think monkey/
lever.

Don't try to win at carnival games either. The carnies don't have
to live in your town and don't need your good will. The smart carnies
gaff (rig) their games to pay off with slum. Slum is the cheap trinket
that isn't worth the price of playing the game. So, it doesn't matter if

you win, you still lose. Fool the weight/age guesser? He doesn't care if he's fooled or not—no matter what, win or lose, you are the fool. Here, take a Kewpie Doll and go away.

There is a very old story. A card shark approaches a young person, like you. He tells you he can make the Jack of Spades jump out of a freshly shuffled deck of cards and squirt cider in your ear.

Do not bet with this man. You will end up with an earful of cider.

23. Stay away from the producers of *Cops* and *Girls Gone Wild* videos

And, above all, if someone hands you a release for a film you appear in, tear it up and run. You are not going to be discovered. (See "You probably aren't going to become a celebrity," above.)

You might want to stay away from all "real life" video productions. First of all they are not real, true, or anything like it. These productions are mounted because they are cheap to make. They employ very little writing and little in the way of sets, have no production values and no actors. Unless multi-million dollar contracts and a piece of the action are offered (they never are) a polite no is in order. I know, the drive to be famous for fifteen minutes overrides common sense every time (see monkey/lever above).

In the same vein (vain?) don't put up Internet pictures or videos that you wouldn't want your mother or minister to see. Better yet, don't put up any pictures at all. In the unlikely event you should become wealthy and famous, extortionists will be paying you a visit.

If you happen to get on one of the so-called "game" television shows with a producer who wants you to "express your emotions," don't be persuaded. This means he/she wants you to do some Tom Cruise couch jumping and mugging for the cameras. Watch some of the shows and ask yourself if you want to give up your dignity for a few bucks—just like those other contestants are doing.

At some future point, clothing may be optional and most people may run around naked. Until that time, it's undoubtedly best to keep your clothes on—at least while cameras are around. If you are thinking that you can get away with streaking, a little shoplifting, or petty crime, remember—your mumsey or daddums may not be watching, but the security cameras are; they never sleep.

Take a pass on any show that has Jerry Springer or Maury Povich as a host as well as the ones that are tell-all rip-offs. You will not become a star; it's far more likely you will become a total schmuck—and everyone else will know about it.

Caution: Showing your boobs isn't worth a string of cheap glass beads, even if you are drunk.

24. Never, ever buy a pony, a horse, a boat, or a swimming pool.

These are the things you typically want in the worst way and when you get them it will probably be in the worst way. A pony, horse, or a dog big enough to fit into the category is a decision to regret as well. These things eat in mass quantities and poop more than they eat. When you ride a horse or pony, you will spend at least half the ride trying to get it away from the barn. Most of these critters spend their time in a field remembering the few times they were ever ridden or visited. The pony-size dogs are tied to a doghouse or locked in a chain-link compound like some condemned criminal. If you aren't emancipated yet—that means you've moved out of mommy and daddy's care and away from their money—don't worry, mumsey and daddums will feed and clean up after your mistake.

A boat is a thing that sits in the marina or carport—much like that pony in the field—for the most part. The other option involves spending money on slip fees and maintenance. The old tale that the happiest day of your life is when you bought it and the very best day is when you sell it holds up, probably better than the motor on the boat.

Actually owning a swimming pool is fraught with problems. See mumsey and daddums for someone to keep chemicals in the water and to clean the pool and maintain the heater and pump. If they cooperate and are willing, your friends will love your pool because their parents filled theirs with dirt long ago, when their kids turned thirteen.

If you insist on the dog, horse, pony, boat, pool experience, go to the phonebook and look up RENTAL.

25. Your opinion has little value.

Didn't want to hear that one, did you? You've been told all your life that everyone has opinions and yours is just as good as any. The folks who told you that lied. How many times have you heard, "That's his opinion." Probably as often as, "That's what they say."

Both statements are essentially worthless.

No one is really interested in your opinion on world economics, foreign policy, the energy crisis, or the safety of atomic reactors. You might give a scientist an insight into what people in your demographic think, but that's about it.

If your opinion was as good as anyone's, we wouldn't need physicians, mechanics, rocket scientists, geologists, or any other expert opinion. You might have an interest in what your art history professor thinks of the works of Michelangelo, but you probably wouldn't ask the janitor. He may have an opinion and you may even be interested in what he has to say, but the janitor is not likely to have the same knowledge, training, or experience required to give a worthwhile opinion.

Now when those commercials in which they ask a "man on the street" what he or she would do about the energy crisis come on, you can change the channel. Unless you are asked, treat your own opinion as if it were like most of the others—nobody wants to hear it.

26. Forget all the teen-speak and jock-talk.

It is typically mental static—know whut I'm sayin'? It's like man, it's really awesomely annoying.

The use of this and other teen-speak may put you in good stead with your peers, but your friends aren't the ones that will hire you or make other life-altering decisions for you.

Include in this, the habit of ending every sentence with a—like man—a tonal change (high-rising terminal) that makes it sound like a question, know whut I'm sayin'? This is also known as the "moronic interrogative," if you'd like to put a label on it. However, President Obama has convinced millions that low-sinking terminals are somehow neat. Listen to the last word in the sentence go down. Kinda' like a slam dunk, ya' know? His low-sinking terminals are a sure clue that he's back at the teleprompter.

For further guidance on idiot-speak, listen to, ya-know—like locker room interviews with jocks. Um, ya know, um, it's really like, ya know whut I'm sayin', um—ya know. You will begin to think Yogi Berra (whoever that guy is) is a great intellect. He once claimed, "I never said half the things I really said."

And, young ladies, the Valley Girl thing is over. It popped up in the 70s long before you were born. It's so yesterday. Get a life.

And African-American friends, what works on the street ain't working in the board room and neither are you if you bring it with you.

Become an intellectual, it's easy. Eliminate two words from

your vocabulary. They are, awesome and whatever. You will be a doozie and will become the cat's pajamas, know whut I'm sayin'? Probably not.

27. Don't argue or fight with cops.

This should be evident to anyone who has ever seen the TV show *Cops*. You might want to watch *Cops* once in a while, just to enhance how you feel about yourself. However, some still try to persuade their arresting officer they are innocent. The cop probably doesn't really care about your story. He's heard them all before anyway. The most common lie used to be, "The check is in the mail." More recently it's become "It's not my dope, my friend left it in the car."

The cop can't decide your guilt or innocence anyway, that's up to the court, so you might as well keep your mouth shut. If you open it, chances are things will become a lot worse rather than a little better—particularly if you are guilty.

Don't try to tell an officer what your rights are. He has them memorized and will tell you what they are while he adjusts the handcuffs. You might prove your level of intelligence to the officer by offering physical resistance. At that point one of several things might happen: You get pepper sprayed, you wind up lying face down on a dirty street in handcuffs, you have the living #@%* knocked out of you via electronic shock, or you suffer a gunshot wound, courtesy of the taxpayers—or all of the above. You will not win the argument or the fight.

If you think you are fighting for honor and respect, forget it. Your friends who see the video of the incident on YouTube will simply be reminded that you are the idiot they thought you were in the first place.

And while you are at it, don't interfere with the work of a repo man.

A hint: If you hear sirens in the distance, put a shirt on. Seems cops have an affinity for arresting shirtless men. If you live in a trailer park, a shirt is a definite plus.

28. Don't try to impress other people.

This isn't to say you shouldn't be an example to them. Trying to impress people with how cool and neat you are is probably futile anyway. The attempt will only verify that you are anything but neat and far from cool.

Take a look at the prison or jail TV shows. These guys/gals have to impress their fellow inmates because if they appear weak or apathetic, they are very likely to become victims.

They adorn their bodies with tattoos, pump, pose, and posture and put on their war face at every opportunity. From time to time they confront authority, just to show their cellmates they are bad and they aren't going to take any crap from "the man." Except for the mind-midgets, of which there are more than a few—after all this is a prison—everyone knows this for what it is and aren't impressed. They know these guys often cry themselves to sleep each night.

Don't try to impress anyone by weirding up either. One look at Marilyn Manson should prove this one. It seems like only yesterday Marilyn walked among us. Sticking steel in your face, tattoos, overweight, underweight, all-black clothing, blue and maroon hair, Mohawks, baggy clothes, underwear over outerwear, partial nudity, crude t-shirts, and publicly passing of gas has all been done to the extent that it is no longer annoying, it's just boring. You just can't do much to weird up anymore anyway. And forget about wearing your hat sideways or backwards, particularly if you are white. This practice is really yesterday and as boring as one of those rhymes (raps) that repeats itself over, and over, and over, and over.

The reason there aren't any more freak shows in carnivals is because all the freaks are now on your side of the tent. Goth goes back to the late 70s, it's so yesterday. Where were you then? Where is Marilyn these days anyway?

29. In much the same vein (ouch)

Piercings will heal and when you are finished being "different" the holes will close and you will once again fit into your new part of the herd. That is unless you have really messed yourself up with ear spools, lip plugs, and other permanently disfiguring body modifications.

Permanent stuff like tattoos and disfigurements are a different matter. Yes, tattoos are relatively permanent, or very difficult and expensive to erase. If you intend to have your neck or face tattooed, you should think about a life in a minimum wage job, the unemployment line, riding to work in the back of a pickup truck, or some other job with your name on your shirt. Keep in mind most of the carnival ride operator positions are already filled.

In the Arthur Penn movie *Bonnie and Clyde*, C.W. Moss's daddy was more upset by the fact he had gotten a tattoo than the fact he was robbing banks and running around with Bonnie and Clyde. (Shows you how far we've come since the Great Depression.)

Maybe they are becoming more acceptable, but few CEOs or professionals—outside the entertainment industry—have their necks or faces tattooed. Fewer still have their arms covered—so far. Maybe tattoos are more acceptable now that grandma has one, but times change, while tattoos stay on to become faded blobs that look like hematomas gone bad. To think, grandma used to be concerned about spider veins on her legs. Now they are just part of the scenery.

Tattoos and weirding up are more attempts to fit in somewhere, as the simpletons claim, "to establish and express our individuality." In fact these radical individualists usually appear to be wearing the uniform of non-uniformity.

No one truly wants to be a non-conformist, or you would see more natty formal attire at anti-war rallies.

30. Avoid crude language

No, this isn't some moral statement or a plea for you to make nice.
It's a plea for you to be cooler.

You see, Lenny Bruce, whoever he was, died so that you could say
any crude thing you like in public. Lenny was a comedian who died
of a drug overdose in the bathroom, much like John Belushi, and
was admired and followed by the likes of Richard Pryor and Eddie
Murphy who inherited his legacy for smutty language acceptance.
All of this began in the 50s and 60s, so it's had a long time to push
the envelope to the point that just about anybody can say anything
anywhere and no one will even bat an eye. Just about all of the late
George Carlin's famous words you can't say on TV are now being
said regularly, at least on satellite radio.

The reason the "words" used to be so great was that they had
shock value. Now using them is like riding a rollercoaster—for the
393rd time. The thrill is long gone. A couple of words are being held
in reserve for special occasions. The Revs Al and Jesse have reserved
the "N" word for the express purpose of getting talk show hosts fired
and for embarrassing any white person who may let it slip out. However, this word can still be used if you are of African descent or are a
member of a Hip Hop organization.

The infamous "F" word still must be used with reservation. This
may be because it sounds Teutonic and guttural, which is to say
"dirty." Anyway, with all of the other "dirty" words to choose from,
it seems this one still gets special attention.

The best reason for not using the "dirty" word, or the ones you
aren't supposed to say is, they just don't have the snap, crackle, and

pop they once did. Remember how your grandparents were shocked when Clark Gable (Rhett Butler) said "Frankly my dear I just don't give a 'D' word," in *Gone With the Wind*? It just doesn't crackle any more.

Where did Rhett go after he left Scarlet and Tara anyway? Frankly, I don't give a "D" word.

31. Recognize that television commercials as well as other forms of advertising affect YOU.

What? Surely not me. I ignore all that stuff, don't you?

Millions are spent on advertising during the Super Bowl and billions are spent each year on just changing your perception of products and services. No advertisement appears by accident. Every major advertiser spends thousands of dollars just to learn if any given advertisement will be effective. Sure, mistakes are made and money is misspent, but very little is spent on the hope an advertising campaign will somehow work.

Why do you want that particular burger or burrito? Why are you buying that brand of soda or beer? Do you really rely on your own opinion or only word-of-mouth information from your friends in selecting the products, services, or entertainment you choose? Perhaps, but the advertisers can give you strong evidence that your choices are definitely affected. Advertisers wouldn't spend the money they do if advertising weren't effective.

32. Tobacco

(See Dope above.) This topic deserves some special treatment because tobacco is legal and easily obtainable by anyone of nearly any age and it is a very dangerous and deadly substance. If you are about 65 or older, you can get a pass on this one, anyone younger than that is open to the charge of being stupid and making a very stupid decision. Those who are older were often told that tobacco was harmless or even good for them. Doctors appeared in advertising to assure them they were doing the right thing. Tobacco companies lied to them about the dangers of smoking.

The rest of you who made the choice to use tobacco did so in the face of overwhelming evidence and an overabundance of caution. "Cigarettes will kill you!"

In spite of the programs, the cautions, the preventable cancers, the emphysema, heart attacks, and the rest that goes with tobacco use, far too many young people think they won't be affected by it. Perhaps the thinking is, it won't happen to me, or—more likely—it won't happen to me now. Besides, when I get old, it won't matter so much.

It may well be the reason young people begin to use tobacco is that they think it will make them appear to be more like adults or it will give them acceptance and stature among their friends.

Most of those old movie stars who looked so cool lighting up, lighting up their girl friend's cigarette and then blowing smoke out of their nose are dead—many of them from lung cancer or other tobacco-related illnesses.

A rational view of the attempt to appear adult and cool is that lighting up will do no such thing. There may be some shock value and it may incur the incredulity of those who care about you. They will be shocked by the fact you are so stupid that you will put your health at risk to do something everyone knows is bad for you—and you are paying good money to do it.

Tobacco is one of the most addictive drugs known. When it is banned in prisons, it becomes even more expensive than crack, heroin, or cocaine. Mark Twain said it best, *"Giving up smoking is the easiest thing in the world. I know because I've done it thousands of times."*

You don't need to get a stamp so that you can stamp STUPID on your forehead, just wave your STUPID flag—your cigarette—as you go by and everyone will know. Too stupid to live and proving it. Don't worry, if recent efforts to legalize marijuana become law, you can take that up as well, and prove you are doubly stupid.

33. Spring break

No, in spite of what the TV guy said, you probably don't deserve one. And because everyone else is going is no reason for you to go. You might be better off going home and getting to know your family a little better. They will still be around after all of those "good" friends have forgotten you exist.

The reason for avoiding Spring Break is most people will go to the beach. This may be an added reason for not going to the beach at all. The beach is nothing more than a fairly narrow strip of sand inhabited by drunks—at least in the strip you are interested in—with salt water on one side and motels, hotels, and condos on the other. Bleached, white old people who shouldn't wear bathing suits and other adults with children who may remind you of your younger siblings may inhabit other strips of sand.

Some beaches allow driving on them, just to provide an extra hazard for pedestrians who, after an hour or two of shooting beers, can't find their way back to either the hotel or the water.

Grit, tar balls, sun, stingrays, sea urchins, jelly fish, nibbling fish, and sharks aren't the only biters; heavy surf, rip tides, glass, errant surfboards, hypothermia, boats, pollution, hypodermic needles—and that's just the water side of things.

The sand part also contains grit, tar balls, doggy doo, sun, glass, and hypodermic needles, but has the added delights of volleyball, would-be athletes going out for passes, errant Frisbee catchers, assorted drunks in random states of drunkenness, people with and without clothing, fights, monster dogs, what they leave, and other assorted obstacles. The added traffic hazards of beach vehicles between the sand and hotel scarcely require mentioning.

On the other side of the beach should be a temporary refuge, but the drunks not on the beach roam the halls looking for or dishing out mayhem in huge portions. The sports of chugging massive quantities and balcony diving have taken over where water sports left off. Wet T-shirt contests, freak dancing, and casual sex with random partners reign. Perverts patrol the hallways looking for sweet young things to slip drugs to on the sly. For those who elude handcuffs, hospital emergency rooms, jail, and the morgue, everyone has what they believe is a great time—excepting those who wake up with a thug or slug in their beds. Amy Winehouse and Dennis Rodman looked so cute last night when the lights were out.

The money you save by avoiding spring break could—well you figure that one out.

34. Go to a place of worship.

I know, I know, you've been told religion is a superstition created by old folks and is intended to keep you in line. All religions are responsible for conflict and the world's woes. Remember, you've also been told other lies as well. By now you should be able to think for yourself a bit.

You will meet likeable people, get involved in activities that aren't self-destructive, and learn that other folks aren't just window dressing and furniture for your world. You may find out that your deity isn't some old geezer with a white beard who sits around on a cloud all day. You may learn it is the men and women who are lost that cause most of the world's problems, not religion.

If the folks in your place of worship tell you that you must force your religion on others, that the world should submit to your way, or that you should kill non-believers—grab your hat and run. If you are old enough to read this, you know the difference between good and evil.

But don't a lot of people go to their place of worship for business contacts, to socialize, and to make themselves feel good? I suppose some do, but at least they go.

Anyway, the NFL games don't start until after noon.

When it comes to choosing a religion, remember only you can choose. Others may influence your choice, but the choice is yours to make. There are lots to choose from. Islamic fascists would force you into their religion at the point of a gun but that would not necessarily make you a true believer of Islam.

The writer, because of any number of reasons, chose Christianity, so I'll use it as an example. There are several 'brands,' sects or denominations of Christianity, but there is one or more that makes the choice a simple one. For the writer at least, simpler is better.

To become a Christian is simply to admit you believe in a higher power—God—and that Christ is your redeemer. That Christ died for you to be redeemed—for you to saved, if you will. You choose to believe that he rose again and because you believe this, you will have an afterlife and live forever with Him in heaven.

Do not wait for someone to prove this to you, or agree with you. It doesn't need to be proven or demonstrated with evidence, logic or reason. Don't argue it out with others from other faiths. If you choose to believe it, that's it—for you. Other Christians, with other 'brands' of religion may not agree with you.

For many Christians, it's that simple. No ceremonies, no sprinkling, no dipping, no chants, no doing good works and no further liturgy.

35. Don't get caught up in the "ME" thing.

The present generation is referred to as the "me" generation. Many have lost sight of the fact they inhabit a world populated by people who are, given a few years or clothing sizes, no different than themselves. Because mommy and daddy told them they were special and the sun wouldn't rise or set if they disappeared, at some point they decided it was all about them. People are not just furniture for your existence.

Of course you have to look out for number one, but making it an obsession is no way to live.

You've been told you are a unique individual. You *are*—just like everyone else out there. You are no different than the rest of the herd. You will eventually die and leave the world just the way you entered it, alone. Hopefully, your family and some friends will remember you passed this way and some may even have something good to say about you.

Very few people, including your best friends, will grieve for more than a month or two after you are gone.

Depressing, ain't it? A helping of the truth usually is.

36. Your culture

This is something you hear a great deal about. It is a greater part
of who and what you are. Without it, you are little or nothing. This is
why it is constantly under attack. Those who would have the world
their way, and want to include your world in it, constantly attack
your culture.

So, let's take a look at the attacks: You have heard that ceremonies, symbols, chants, prayers, and religion are of no consequence.
Ceremonies are silly exercises and religion is mysticism and magic
for simpletons. Symbols such as the flag, the cross, the crescent, or
star are meaningless. Chants or prayers are ineffective.

If all of this is true, why is it so important for you to be taught otherwise? Brainwashers spend an inordinate amount of time attempting
to separate their victims from their culture. These symbols, incanta-
tions, and the rest are what hold us all together.

According to "culturists" some cultures are better than others. If
you are white and of European extraction for example, your culture
is at the very least questionable. It's those other cultures that that are
rich in tradition and their culture should be preserved. Claiming the
moral high ground of "diversity," these so-called culturists never
look inward to their own bigotry.

37. The religion of diversity

In the late 20th Century educationalists and others found that the term "diversity" had a nice ring to it. They saw it as an answer to racial inequality, gender issues, and ethnic problems. Diversity is one of those ideas that has a warm and fuzzy public relations ring to it. However, sports teams learned early on that diversity has to take a back seat to talent if you are going to have a winning team. There are few organizations that are less diverse than sports teams. Winning trumps most other stuff and I'm not interested in the diversity of my surgical team, just their ability and talent.

38. America is a racist nation

If you hear this old canard you should ask the person telling it to offer some evidence of it. Usually they will mention long-gone slavery, Jim Crow laws, or some other practice from the 20th Century. They think of racism as a black and white issue. Yellow, brown, or red just don't compute. If you mention 1954 or Brown v. The Board of Education, they will go... wha?

You should begin with listing the thousands of success stories of minority members who have made it. You might even mention that a large majority of Americans voted for an African-American president and the vast number of successful minority politicians, sports figures, entertainers, and business people. You might also mention the millions of minority millionaires. These folks would never make it in a society that is truly racist.

Admittedly, there are racist individuals among us, but where symptoms of it exist, it is more often class discrimination rather than skin color that drives it. No one wants to live next to a gangster, no matter what his race happens to be.

Discrimination has gotten a bad rap but we do it every day. Go to an American Idol try-out or a nightclub where the potential customers line up and hope to be admitted along with the other cool people. Or, simply go to a job interview or casting call. You will see discrimination in its purest form.

Put your talent out there in the marketplace and watch discrimination in action. And, if you aren't a member of the herd, get ready for all-out discrimination.

39. Our Constitution guarantees separation of Church and State

Anyway, that's what we are told. If you listen to current wisdom, the Constitution only means whatever the Supreme Court interprets its meaning to be. Some politicians claim your Constitution is a work in progress and that it grows and changes as needed. This is like saying the contract you sign can be changed when the other party to the agreement decides to change it. The function of the Constitution is to limit the powers of government, not to facilitate it.

> The First Amendment (BILL OF RIGHTS)
> *Congress shall make no law respecting an establishment of religion, or prohibiting the free exercise thereof; or abridging the freedom of speech, or of the press; or the right of the people peaceably to assemble, and to petition the Government for a redress of grievances.*

It's a far reach from not enacting a law establishing a religion to where we have come regarding the so-called separation of Church and State. You can see that the Supreme Court seems to question the "free exercise" part of the amendment with their ban on prayer in schools and other separation rulings and legislation.

What the founders—mostly Christian and Deist men—intended was to keep the Government out of the religion business. They didn't want a state religion. Saudi Arabia, and most other Arab countries have state religions based on Islam. Many Middle Eastern countries, such as Saudi Arabia, forbid religions other than Islam by law. Many of them are governed by Islamic law, Sharia.

The Constitution requires only that no religion is recognized as a state religion. Other issues of church and state have been matters of judicial decisions and case law without regard to the Constitution.

From time to time, you will hear someone say that they have "rights." Usually they are referring to the Bill of Rights in the Constitution. Sometimes you will hear "They can't do that, the Constitution says…" The sad truth is, the Constitution and your rights are what whoever is in power at any given time declares what it says—or interprets its meaning to be.

Daniel Isaac Morris

40. Feminism and feminist groups are formed to protect women's rights.

This is another one of those "everyone says" myths. Admittedly, there is a degree of truth to it. All good myths require a degree of truth to make them believable.

Stories about how Mr. Rogers was a patriotic warrior are always made believable by including his story along with one of a real war hero. Fred Rogers was never in the military and never saw battle, but the myth that he was a Navy Seal lives on.

Feminism and the National Organization of Women (NOW) are ostensibly bastions to protect the rights of all women. The only problem is, they are preoccupied with protecting leftist causes.

Avowed conservative Sarah Palin was wrung out and left to dry by not only her opponents, but also by her so-called feminist sisters who applauded as she twisted slowly in the wind.

She was attacked for having a job while she had children. Until Sarah, feminists frothed at the mouth at the mention of a working mother being anything but heroic in Athenian proportions. They would have been appalled at any pejorative mention of one of their sisters' children. If it were revealed that she had a child who had a baby out of wedlock, this fact would have been celebrated and the mother paraded and bedecked with laurel.

So-called feminists will jump to defend the worst of anti-feminism and abuse, if the offender is a leftist radical, progressive, or liberal.

So, even the feminists had to admit what everyone suspected all along, NOW and their ilk weren't so much interested in women's rights or even feminism, they were interested in furthering a progressive, leftist agenda. If the progressive woman was in need of defending, so much the better. However, it's clear that conservatives, people who don't have the same values or ideas of the left, need not apply.

It's not that there is something wrong with progressives. It's the methods some of them use and their subterfuge that stink.

41. Economics

As we indicated in an earlier chapter, it is most likely that your education has not included basic economic theory. Whether or not that is the case, you should, independently if necessary, educate yourself in basic economic theories. Make sure you choose those that agree with common sense and reject those that have been proven unworkable. No matter what experts tell you, you will undoubtedly find that Marxist theories have a very poor record of improving people's lives.

Be prepared to hear a lot of harebrained schemes. A lot depends on keeping you in the dark concerning economics. Don't believe anything that doesn't pass the smell test. If it sounds too good to be true—well, by now, you know how to fill in the rest.

Don't expect much help from government experts. They tend to talk in trillions of dollars. Most people you know have no idea how much a billion dollars is, let alone a trillion. These are figures no one encounters in day-to-day experience.

Educate yourself on the concepts of credit and interest. Know the difference between APR, APY, EAR, and a whole range of other initials and acronyms that are intended to keep you in the dark and confused. Billions of dollars are invested in keeping you ignorant. The federal government has made it a life calling.

Don't get a credit card until you have a steady, predictable income. Credit card companies make millions by handing out a piece of plastic with the inference that you can have anything you want at any time. They make much more when you don't have the means to pay off the card. You will be stuck with exorbitant interest and penalties.

Don't be sucked into paying only the minimum payment! This ensures a lifetime of servitude to the credit card company.

If you need to buy a high-ticket item, think about it. Do you really need it? The very best way to buy that item is to save up for it. This eliminates paying interest and you may even negotiate a lower price when you tell the clerk you are paying cash. Credit card companies collect from the seller and the buyer, so the store will gain two or more percent when you pay cash.

If you still have to buy the item, don't buy it on a credit card. Mooch off of your parents or other family members. Or, ask them if you can "borrow" the money from them. Failing that, ask your friends for a loan and offer to pay them interest. It will be cheaper than the credit card deal and your friend might appreciate a chance to make a little extra cash.

At all costs, don't cash one of those checks the credit card companies send in the mail. Don't borrow against your credit card account either. Both of these rip-offs carry high interest rates.

Avoid "Cash Advance" or the so-called payday loan. It will be your loan and their payday. These loans require exorbitant interest rates that push the envelope of usury. You may have to take out another loan just to pay the interest and fees.

42. Student Loans

This is so important it requires another chapter. It would be easy to simply advise that you don't even think about student loans. However, if mumsey and daddums can be relied upon to pay off the loan, it's something to think about. If you can talk someone else into making the payments, or if you're independently wealthy, it's something to consider. However, this may also mean that you don't need a student loan.

First of all, a college education is highly over-rated. You may have to work for years in a low-paying job to pay off your college education while you struggle to make ends meet. A college degree is a benefit only if you can afford it.

What follows is admittedly controversial. Only upper-class, well-to-do kids went to college before the G.I. Bill came into being after WWII. The G.I. Bill introduced something new into higher education—government money and federal regulations. Need evidence of the government's need for control? The government even tried to regulate colleges who would not accept federal dollars. Subsidized education opened the doors of academe to people who weren't qualified previously. Colleges had to reduce entrance standards in order to attract students who now had the wherewithall to pay for college. (Can you say OPEN DOOR?) Soon campuses were awash in students, some capable, some incapable of finding their way to a classroom.

A father argued to an older college professor, "My son has a 'B' average and is on the Dean's list."

"You had better hope so," said the professor. "If he didn't have a

'B' average, it would indicate he is somewhat mentally challenged.

43. War

You will probably hear more lies and myths on this subject than any other. This is not to say there aren't some truths about it.

No one wants to engage in war, and no one except a few psychopaths like war. This makes it the purview of warm and fuzzy romantic types who claim the moral high ground because they and they alone dislike war. These warm and fuzzies often claim conservatives want and enjoy war. Some of these folks claim America should never go to war—even when attacked.

"War is hell." – William Tecumseh Sherman

Sherman was renowned as a fierce—some would say tyrannical—military leader, and in September 1864 he gave orders for the city of Atlanta to be evacuated and burned. Despite appeals from the citizens of Atlanta, including reminders that there were elderly and pregnant women whom it would be difficult and even perilous to move, Sherman's decision was final

Not since WWII has American truly been at war. In fact, war hasn't been declared since that time. And, some would say, America hasn't fought to win a war since then. Wars have been "military or police actions" that are run by politicians to gain political advantage. Many political leaders want the war on terrorism to be a police action in which enemy combatants are treated as criminals with civil rights, rather than enemy soldiers. Since WWII, which the U.S. entered when the Japanese attacked this country, every war has been preemptive."

Hitler never attacked the U.S. mainland. William Jefferson Clinton led a preemptive war in Serbia. President Clinton's second secretary

of state most forcefully articulated the philosophy that dictators for-
feit their sovereignty rights if they mistreat their people. "America,"
said Madeleine Albright, "is the indispensable nation that must lead
a coalition of the willing to dislodge dictators such as Slobodan
Milosevic in Serbia." These are facts the critics of George W. Bush
somehow missed.

Technically speaking, the Iraq war was simply a renewal of
hostilities, not a new war. All of these arguments are moot now. We
"invaded" the Balkans, we struck Iraq. We did so with no intention
of "winning." We wanted a regime change and to make a political
settlement.

We fought WWII to win. Thousands of "innocent" casualties were
accepted. There was no attempt to win the hearts and minds of the
people. The goal in WWII was the conquest of the enemy by any
means—including atomic warfare. Over 70,000 people died immedi-
ately on impact of "Little Boy", the first atom bomb, when it struck
Hiroshima, Japan. The war was Shermanesque. Cities, along with
their civilian populations were bombed into oblivion. No one cared
about the hearts and minds in Hiroshima or Nagasaki. They were
targets that stood in the way of unconditional surrender. They were
bombed to shorten the war and save American lives.

Should you join up and "fight for freedom?" Should you listen
to the old men who want to send you into harm's way? It may be
something to consider if you need an education or a job; however,
you should enter into it with your eyes wide open.

Wars initially begin with lots of patriotism, flag waving and assur-
ances they will be short-lived.

Vietnam War, 116 months
American Revolution, 100 months
U.S. Civil War, 48 months
World War II, 45 months
Korean War, 37 months

Iraq War—counting
Afghanistan—counting

Few of our wars were as short as predicted. The Civil War, one of the shortest, was predicted to be over in a few weeks.

As a war grinds on, particularly the ones in which we have no intention of winning, support for the war wanes. As support for the war effort fades, so does support for those fighting the war. The public lined the streets for a chance to spit on troops returning from Vietnam. Even when they won a battle—the Tet Offensive—they lost it at home. The American heroes, the troops, might have won the war, but the politicians and the folks at home wanted to cut and run, just as the Democrat leadership wanted to do in the middle of the Iraq war. The Iraq war has been fought to gain political advantage for one party or the other. As the war ground on, George W. Bush's vows of vengeance for the 9/11 attacks faded along with the memory of the 3,017 people who died.

So, if you wish, join up, just make sure you know what you are in for.

"War is hell." Why? If you intend to win any war, it should be hell.

44. Old age

If you aren't there yet, you will be if you are lucky. Chances are you will live to be close to eighty years old. That is unless some politician finally figures out a way to impose socialized medicine and they figure out you cost too much to maintain and are no longer a productive member of society.

Euthanasia is a moderate-sounding term for killing off folks who a) wish to die, b) are no longer contributing, or c) are dissidents. In case you don't think this can happen, some states have already passed legislation to permit "mercy killing," another term for euthanasia. If you believe life begins before the delivery of a baby, abortion is another form of legal euthanasia.

"[The god of healing] did not want to lengthen out good-for-nothing lives... Those who are diseased in their bodies, [physicians] leave to die, and the corrupt and incurable souls they will put an end to themselves." – Plato, The Republic

If you are under thirty, you are encouraged to believe you will never grow old or, and even more insidiously, that you will either not die, or will die much later. Governments are presently kicking their debt and profligate spending further and further down the road for future generations to pay—at some future time.

45. You don't need a nanny.

If you are old enough to read this, you probably don't need a nanny. However, there are a number of people who insist that your government should be a nanny state—a government that will provide for you from the cradle to the grave. Much of Western Europe has adopted the nanny state mode and the radical left in America seems more than willing to impose it in the United States.

It may sound like a good idea at first, but since you should be able to think for yourself by now—do it. It should be insulting for anyone to suggest that the state can take better care of you than you can by yourself.

One of the best examples of the failure of cradle-to-the-grave care can be found right here. Before America's indigenous people learned they had the right to fleece everyone in casinos, they lived a life subsidized by the government.

So-called Indian reservations provided a carefree life where no one had to work and their basic needs were taken care of. This, of course, led to a life of government control and self-indulgence.

People who have their every need provided for often fall victim to self-indulgence, alcohol-drugs, and suicide. Remember the list of celebrities in an earlier chapter? Reservations became communities of the depressed, the addicted, the hopeless, and the suicidal.

However, reservations were the answer to the government's need, a need to control the indigenous American population. The same technique was used in the so-called "Great Society" of the Lyndon Johnson era. Much of the African-American population was controlled, made dysfunctional, and ghettoized by the proven process of providing "welfare."

When you become independent, emancipate yourself from parental control. The evidence is clear. If you continue to allow yourself to be kept, you will become depressed, addicted, hopeless, and suicidal.

How many folks do you know who are adults who live with their parents? Or, should we say live off their parents. If you don't control your own destiny, you may die, or live to regret it.

Since the underpinnings of the nanny state are taxes, it can't exist for any long period of time anyway. Soon, everyone is being subsidized and no one is working to pay for it.

For all its warm, cozy, touchy/feely intent, the nanny state is socialistic or even communistic and will, whether intended to or not, devolve into totalitarianism. Nanny states require central planning and control. A government that provides—for example, health care— is a government that will demand control over all aspects of your life so that it can provide that care.

Margaret Thatcher said it best, "Freedom is not synonymous with an easy life. ... There are many difficult things about freedom: It does not give you safety, it creates moral dilemmas for you; it requires self-discipline; it imposes great responsibilities; but such is the nature of Man and in such consists his glory and salvation." And, "The problem with socialism is that eventually you run out of other people's money."

The end: So, where does all this advice lead us?

I suppose one conclusion might be that anyone who has not had a father, or has a father who is missing, or one that is too absorbed in struggling to make it through the day, should find one.

But moreover, that relying on others for guidance and critical thinking may help initially, but the ultimate conclusion is...

FIND YOURSELF.

You are the only person you will live with every day for your entire lifetime.

The following quotes are from various sources. Hopefully you will recognize some of them.

"Becoming a father is easy enough, but being one can be very rough."

"It doesn't matter who my father was; it matters who I remember he was."

"It is a wise child that knows his own father."

"A father's words are like a thermostat that sets the temperature in the house."

"If the new American father feels bewildered and even defeated, let him take comfort from the fact that whatever he does in any fathering situation has a fifty percent chance of being right."

"Blessed indeed is the man who hears many gentle voices call him father!"

"When one has not had a good father, one must create one."

"I cannot think of any need in childhood as strong as the need for a father's protection."

"When I was a boy of 14, my father was so ignorant I could hardly stand to have the old man around. But when I got to be 21, I was astonished at how much the old man had learned in seven years."

Daniel Isaac Morris

Daniel I. Morris is a retired college professor, newspaper
publisher, artist, and writer. He lives with his wife Barbara
in Southwestern Pennsylvania and they winter in central
Florida.

Daniel Isaac Morris

www.ingramcontent.com/pod-product-compliance
Lightning Source LLC
Chambersburg PA
CBHW071640050426
42443CB00026B/775